WORDS OF WISDOM

ABRAHAM LINCOLN

JOLLYJOY

100 Selected Quotes
by Abraham Lincoln

Edition 2024

Published by

JOLLYJOY

G/F, 4771/23, Bharat Ram Road, Daryaganj, New Delhi-110002

E-mail: Contact@jollyjoybooks.com

ISBN: 9789363970007
Cover, Typesetting, and Book Design by JollyJoy
Printed & bound in India

ABOUT THE AUTHOR

Abraham Lincoln (born February 12, 1809, near Hodgenville, Kentucky, U.S.—died April 15, 1865, Washington, D.C.) was the 16th president of the United States (1861–65), who preserved the Union during the American Civil War and brought about the emancipation of enslaved people in the United States. Lincoln and his cabinet U.S. Pres. Abraham Lincoln (seated center) and his cabinet, with Lieut. Gen. Winfield Scott, in the council chamber at the White House, lithograph, 1866. Abraham Lincoln: statue at the Lincoln MemorialStatue of Abraham Lincoln at the Lincoln Memorial, Washington, D.C.

100 SELECTED QUOTES

"Folks are usually about as happy as they make their minds up to be."

WHATEVER
YOU
ARE
BE
A
GOOD
ONE

"Do I not destroy my enemies when I make them my friends?"

"America will never be destroyed from the outside.
If we falter and lose our freedoms,
it will be because we destroyed ourselves."

"My Best Friend is a person who will give me a book I have not read."

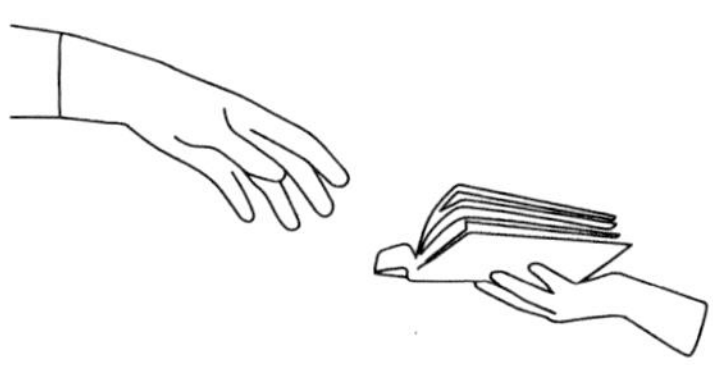

"My concern is not whether God is on our side;
my greatest concern is to be on God's side,
for God is always right."

“I’m a success today because I had a friend who believed in me and I didn’t have the heart to let him down.”

"Books serve to show a man that those original thoughts of his aren't very new after all."

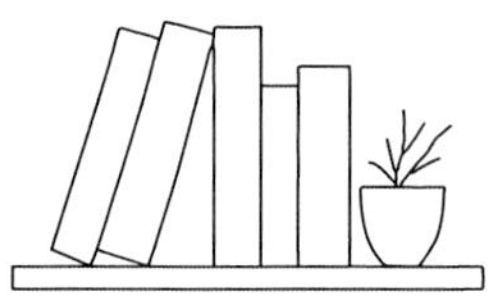

*"When I do good, I feel good.
When I do bad, I feel bad.
That's my religion."*

"Those who deny freedom to others, deserve it not for themselves"

"I am a slow walker,
but I never walk back."

*"Whenever I hear anyone arguing for slavery,
I feel a strong impulse to see
it tried on him personally."*

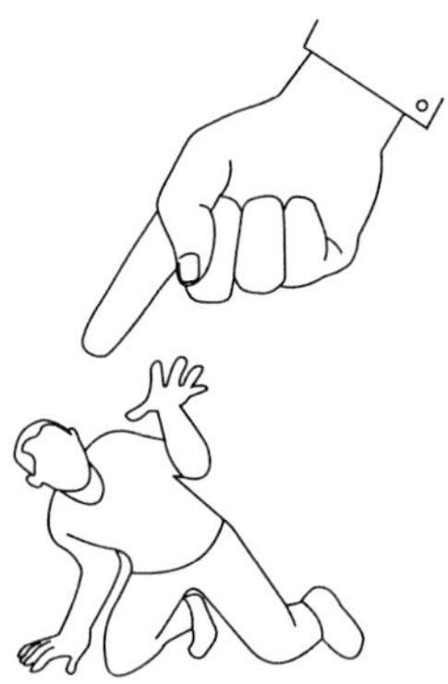

"There are no bad pictures;
that's just how your face looks sometimes."

"I can see how it might be possible for a man to look down upon the earth and be an atheist, but I cannot conceive how a man could look up into the heavens and say there is no God."

"Those who look for the bad in people will surely find it."

"I don't like that man.
I must get to know him better."

*"I am not bound to win, but I am bound to be true.
I am not bound to succeed, but I am bound to live up
to what light I have."*

"When you reach the end of your rope,
tie a knot and hang on."

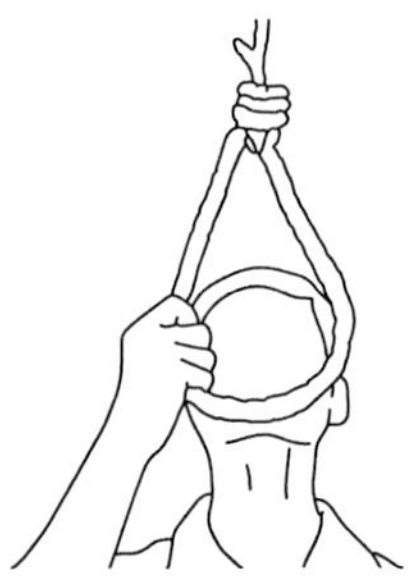

*"You can fool some of the people all of the time,
and all of the people some of the time,
but you can not fool all of the
people all of the time."*

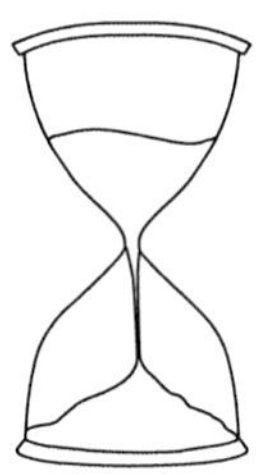

"I would rather be a little nobody,
then to be a evil somebody."

"Be sure you put your feet in the right place,
then stand firm."

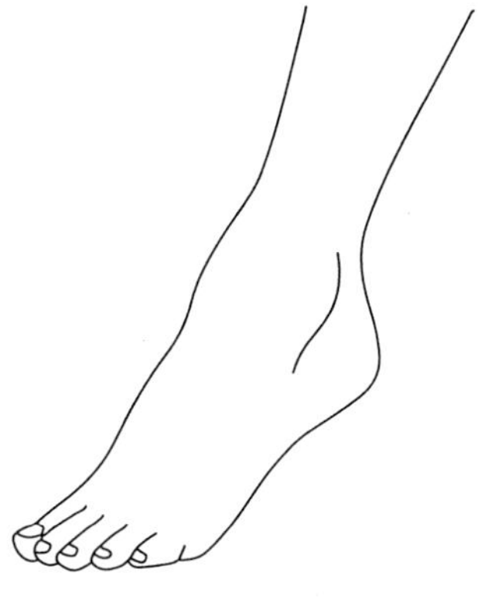

"I have been driven many times upon my knees by the overwhelming conviction that I had no where else to go. My own wisdom and that of all about me seemed insufficient for that day."

*"If I were two-faced,
would I be wearing this one?"*

"All that I am or ever hope to be,
I owe to my angel mother."

"Character is like a tree and reputation its shadow.
The shadow is what we think it is and
the tree is the real thing."

"Always bear in mind that your own resolution to succeed is more important than any one thing."

"The best way to predict your future is to create it."

"No man is poor who has a Godly mother."

"We are not enemies, but friends.
We must not be enemies.
Though passion may have strained,
it must not break our bonds of affection.
The mystic chords of memory will swell when again touched,
as surely they will be, by the better angels of our nature."

"I laugh because I must not cry,
that is all, that is all."

"Give me six hours to chop down a tree and I will spend the first four sharpening the axe."

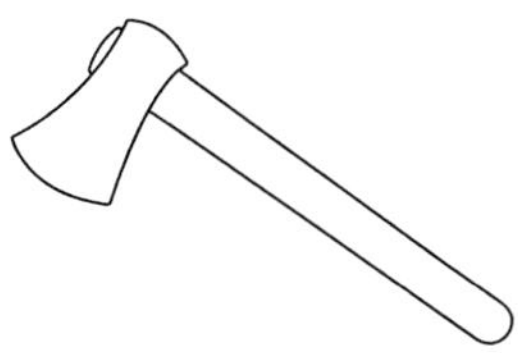

"Tact: the ability to describe others as they see themselves."

"I will prepare and some day
my chance will come."

"Elections belong to the people.
It's their decision. If they decide to turn their back on the fire and burn their behinds, then they will just have to sit on their blisters."

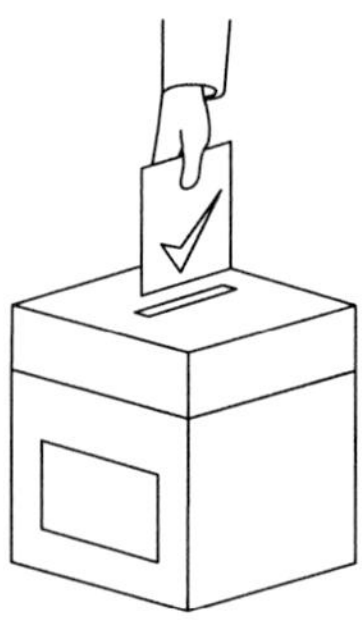

"No man has a good enough memory to be a successful liar"

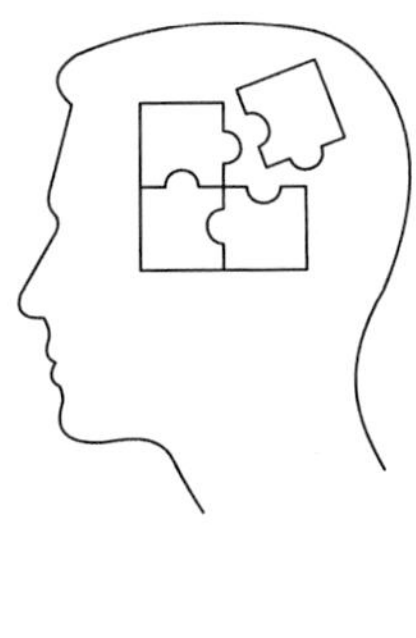

"The best thing about the future is that it comes one day at a time."

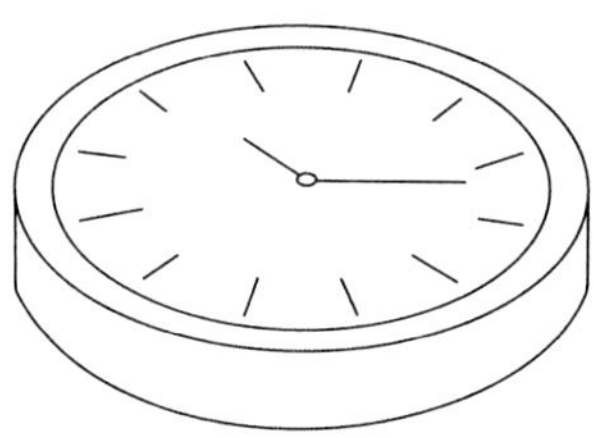

"I have always found that mercy bears richer fruits than strict justice."

*"My father taught me to work, but not to love it.
I never did like to work, and I don't deny it.
I'd rather read, tell stories, crack jokes,
talk, laugh -- anything but work."*

"If you once forfeit the confidence of your fellow citizens,
you can never regain their respect and esteem.
It is true that you may fool all of the people some of the time;
you can even fool some of the people all of the time;
but you can't fool all of the people all of the time.

"All I have learned, I learned from books."

*"Things may come to those who wait,
but only the things left by those who hustle."*

"I care not for a man's religion whose dog and cat are not the better for it."

"You cannot escape the responsibility of tomorrow by evading it today."

EVERY
MAN'S
HAPPINESS
IS
HIS
OWN
RESPONSIBILITY

"I am in favor of animal rights as well as human rights. That is the way of a whole human being."

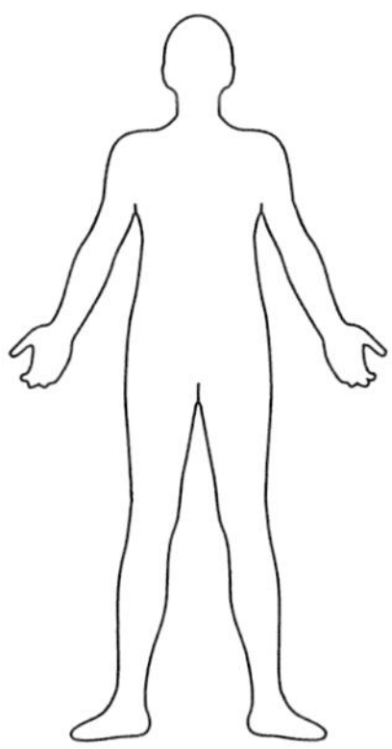

"I do not think much of a man who is not wiser today than he was yesterday."

"It's not me who can't keep a secret.
It's the people I tell that can't."

"In this sad world of ours, sorrow comes to all; and,
to the young, it comes with bitterest agony,
because it takes them unawares.
The older have learned to ever expect it.
I am anxious to afford some alleviation of your present
distress. Perfect relief is not possible, except with time.
You can not now realize that you will ever feel better.
Is not this so? And yet it is a mistake.
You are sure to be happy again. To know this, which is
certainly true, will make you some less miserable now.
I have had experience enough to know what I say;
and you need only to believe it, to feel better at once."

*"The Lord prefers common-looking people.
That is why he made so many of them."*

"It has been my experience that folks who have no vices have very few virtues."

"You have to do your own growing no matter how tall your grandfather was."

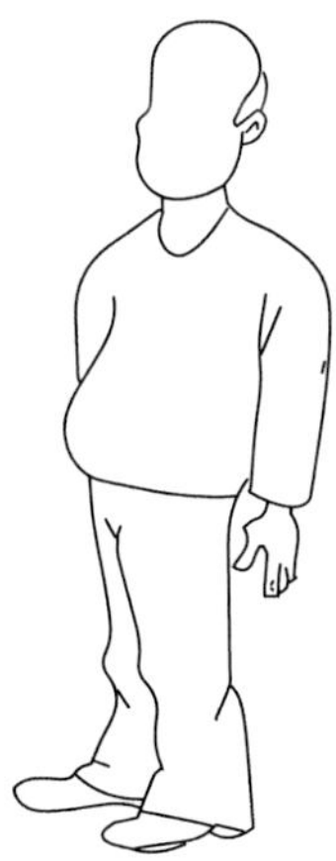

"You cannot help people permanently by doing for them, what they could and should do for themselves."

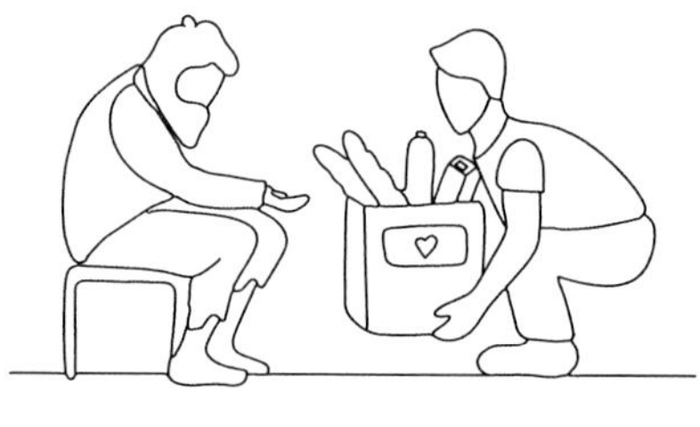

"You can tell the greatness of a man by what makes him angry"

"If this is coffee, please bring me some tea;
but if this is tea, please bring me some coffee."

"I am a firm believer in the people. If given the truth, they can be depended upon to meet any national crisis. The great point is to bring them the real facts, and beer."

"I am not concerned that you have fallen
I am concerned that you arise."

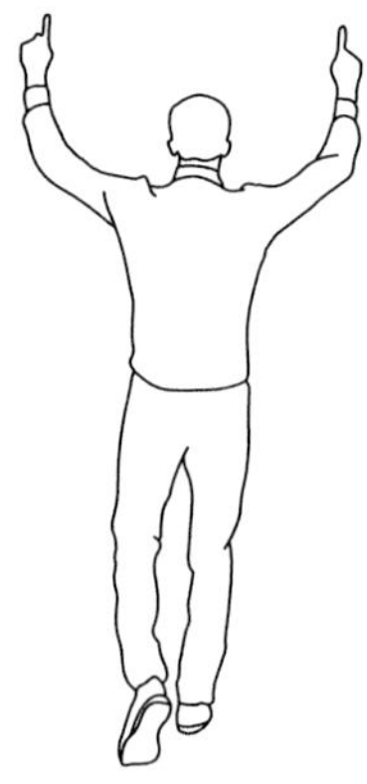

"It is difficult to make a man miserable while he feels worthy of himself and claims kindred to the great God who made him."

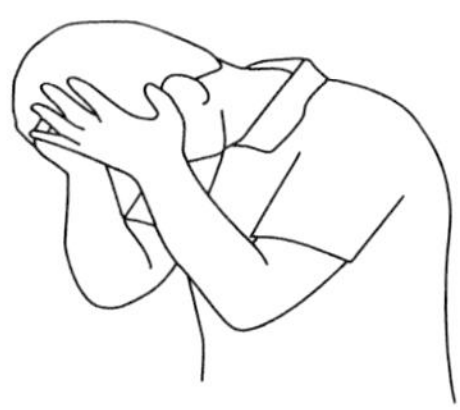

"A house divided against itself cannot stand."
I believe this government cannot endure,
permanently half slave and half free.
I do not expect the Union to be dissolved I do not expect
the house to fall but I do expect it will cease to be divided.
It will become all one thing or all the other."

"I don't know who my grandfather was;
I am much more concerned to know
what his grandson will be."

"To ease another's heartache is to forget one's own."

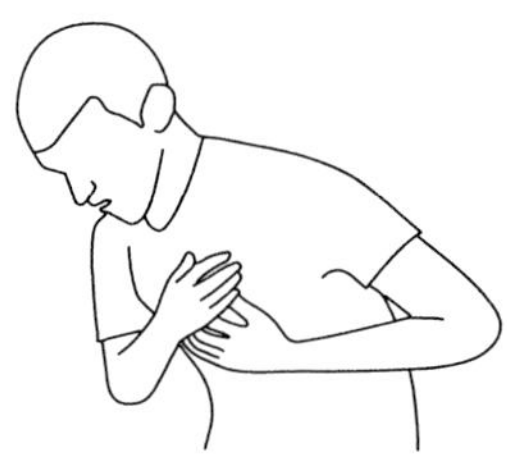

"The better part of one's life consists of his friendships."

"The probability that we may fail in the struggle ought not to deter usfrom the support of a cause we believe to be just."

"As a nation, we began by declaring that 'all men are created equal.' We now practically read it 'all men are created equal, except negroes.' When the Know Nothings get control, it will read 'all men are created equal, except negroes, and foreigners, and Catholics.' When it comes to this I should prefer emigrating to some country where they make no pretense of loving liberty – to Russia, for instance, where despotism can be taken pure, and without the base alloy of hypocrisy."

"When I get ready to talk to people,
I spend two thirds of the time thinking what
they want to hear and one third thinking
about what I want to say."

ACHIEVEMENT
HAS
NO
COLOR

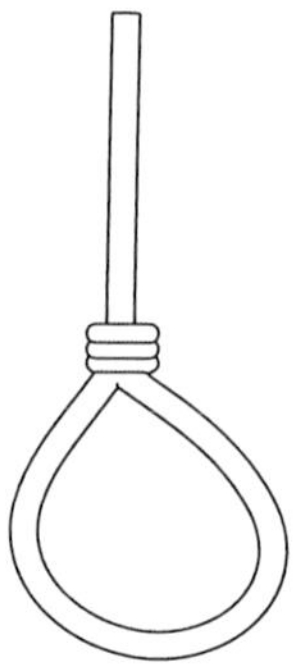

"From whence shall we expect the approach of danger? Shall some trans Atlantic military giant step the earth and crush us at a blow? Never. All the armies of Europe and Asia...could not by force take a drink from the Ohio River or make a track on the Blue Ridge in the trial of a thousand years. No, if destruction be our lot we must ourselves be its author and finisher. As a nation of free men we will live forever or die by suicide."

"Be with a leader when he is right,
stay with him when he is still right,
but, leave him when he is wrong."

"Fourscore and seven years ago our fathers brought forth on this continent, a new nation, conceived in Liberty, and dedicated to the proposition that all men are created equal."

"I do the very best I know how, the very best I can, and I mean to keep on doing so until the end."

*"No matter how much the cats fight,
there always seem to be plenty of kittens."*

"We should be too big to take offense and too noble to give it."

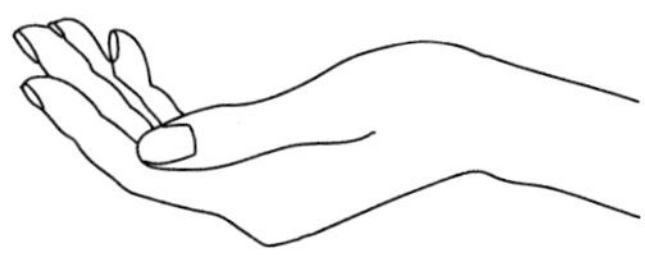

"The Bible is not my book nor Christianity my profession. I could never give assent to the long, complicated statements of Christian dogma."

"If there is anything that links the human to the divine,
it is the courage to stand by a principle
when everybody else rejects it."

"I have come to the conclusion never again to think of marrying, and for this reason, I can never be satisfied with anyone who would be blockhead enough to have me."

THE
BALLOT
IS
STRONGER
THAN
THE
BULLET

*"You can have anything you want if you want it badly enough.
You can be anything you want to be,
do anything you set out to accomplish if you hold to
that desire with singleness of purpose."*

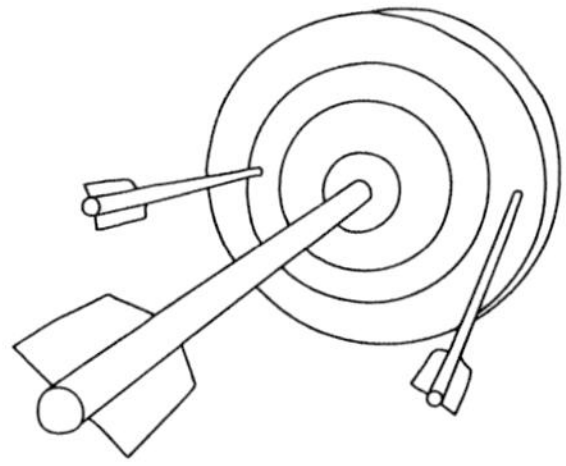

"The greatest fine art of the future will be the making of a comfortable living from a small piece of land."

"As I would not be a slave, so I would not be a master. This expresses my idea of democracy."

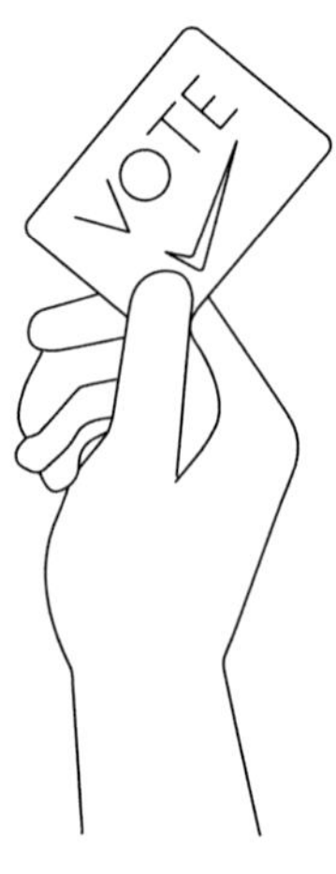

"My great concern is not whether you have failed, but whether you are content with your failure."

"Hypocrite: The man who murdered his parents, and then pleaded for mercy on the grounds that he was an orphan."

"Honor to the soldier and sailor everywhere, who bravely bears his country's cause. Honor, also to the citizen who cares for his brother in the field and serves, as he best can, the same cause."

"Don't criticize them; they are just what we would be under similar circumstances."

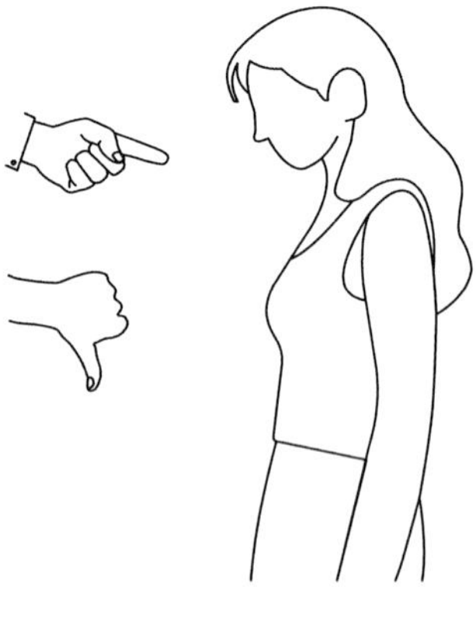

"With malice toward none, with charity for all, with firmness in the right as God gives us to see the right, let us strive on to finish the work we are in, to bind up the nation's wounds, to care for him who shall have borne the battle and for his widow and his orphan, to do all which may achieve and cherish a just and lasting peace among ourselves and with all nations."

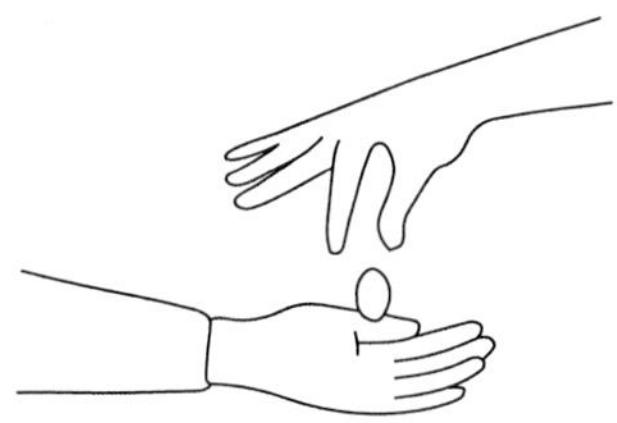

"Get books, sit yourself down anywhere,
and go to reading them yourself."

"Die when I may, I want it said of me by those who knew me best, that I always plucked a thistle and planted a flower where I thought a flower would grow."

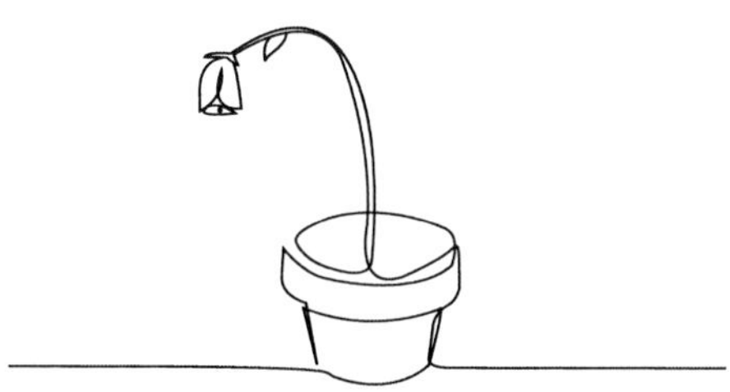

*"If this country is ever demoralized,
it will come from trying to live without work."*

"It is said an Eastern monarch once charged his wise men to invent him a sentence to be ever in view, and which should be true and appropriate in all times and situations. They presented him the words, "And this too, shall pass away." How much it expresses! How chastening in the hour of pride! How consoling in the depths of affliction!"

"Stand with anyone that is right; stand with him while he is right and part with him when he goes wrong."

"You cannot build character and courage
by taking away people's initiative and independence"

"Those who deny freedom to others deserve it not for themselves, and, under a just God cannot retain it."

"Take all that you can of this book upon reason,
and the balance on faith,
and you will live and die a happier man. (When a skeptic
expressed surprise to see him reading a Bible)"

"Let no feeling of discouragement prey upon you, and in the end you are sure to succeed."

"Those who write clearly have readers,
those who write obscurely have commentators."

"Determine that the thing can and shall be done and then... find the way."

"Our safety, our liberty,
depends upon preserving the Constitution of the United States as our fathers made it inviolate.
The people of the United States are the rightful masters of both Congress and the courts, not to overthrow the Constitution, but to overthrow the men who pervert the Constitution."

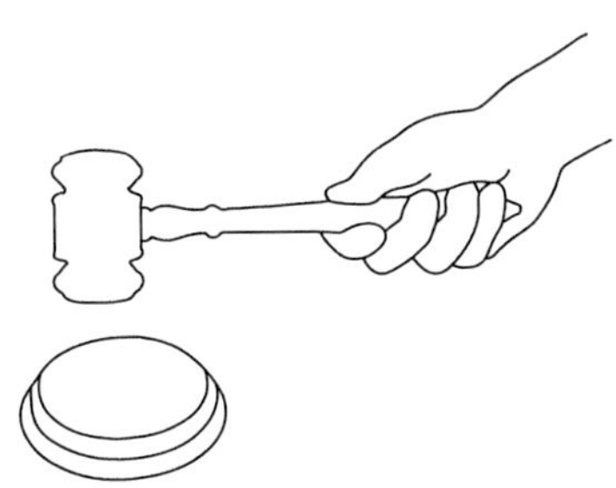

I want in all cases to do right,
and most particularly so,
in all cases with women.

"The dogmas of the quiet past are inadequate to
the stormy present.
The occasion is piled high with difficulty and
we must rise with the occasion. As our case is new,
we must think anew and act anew.
We must disenthrall ourselves,
and then we shall save our country."

"Republicans are for both the man and the dollar, but in case of conflict the man before the dollar."

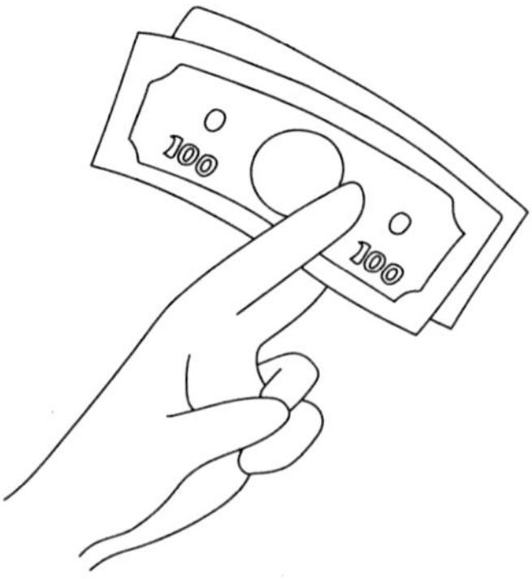

"Don't interfere with anything in the Constitution.
That must be maintained,
for it is the only safeguard of our liberties."

"We the people are the rightful masters of both Congress and the courts, not to overthrow the Constitution but to overthrow the men who pervert the Constitution."

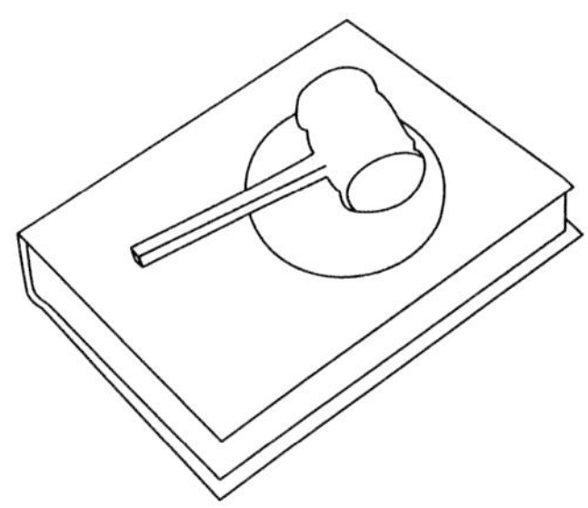